T0041633

THE
dutch oven
COOKBOOK

DEVELOPED BY

WILLIAMS SONOMA

TEST KITCHEN

Photographs Aubrie Pick

weldon**owen**

Contents

Cooking with Dutch Ovens

Cherished by home cooks and professional chefs alike for its versatility and reliability, the dutch oven is an essential piece of cookware for any well-equipped kitchen. Originally used for cooking outdoors over a campfire, dutch ovens have become workhorses in the modern kitchen. In the Williams Sonoma Test Kitchen, where we develop hundreds of recipes every year, we reach for our dutch ovens time and again to make soups and stews, braise meats, cook one-pot meals, and even bake breads and desserts. We love our dutch ovens because they always deliver a perfectly cooked dish. These stylish pots are also well suited for stove-to-table serving and entertaining.

Durability and consistency
Cast-iron dutch ovens are heavier and thicker than stockpots and are deeper than skillets, so they can accommodate a large cut of meat along with vegetables and cooking liquid. Because cast iron conducts and retains heat exceptionally well, dutch ovens are ideal for the long, slow cooking required for stews and braises. The ingredients can be first sautéed or browned and then simmered or braised, all in the same pot. The tight-fitting lid of a dutch oven prevents evaporation—indispensable for successful braising. And with their high sides, dutch ovens are an excellent choice for cooking pasta and deep-frying.

Different sizes and styles
Dutch ovens are available in round and oval shapes, and in traditional uncoated black cast iron and enameled cast iron in vibrant colors, including red, blue, and green. Dutch ovens

that feature an enameled interior require no seasoning and won't react with acidic ingredients. The enamel coating resists rusting, chipping, and scratching and is easy to clean. Capacities range from 1 quart to 9½ quarts; a dutch oven that holds 5, 6, or 7 quarts will be suitable for most home cooks. The classic form and feel of these pots make them showpieces that can go from stove top to oven to table for serving. Because of their longevity and timeless beauty, dutch ovens make wonderful wedding gifts and often become prized family heirlooms, passed down from one generation of cooks to the next.

Versatility in the kitchen

From the homey to the sophisticated, from main course to dessert, the recipes in this book demonstrate the dutch oven's versatility. Summer Vegetable Lasagne cooks evenly and stays moist, thanks to the pot's tall sides and uniform heat conduction. From searing the meatballs to simmering the sauce, all of the steps of Curried Meatballs with Spicy Tomato Sauce can be done in a single pot. For another comforting one-pot meal (perfect for easy cleanup), try Cider-Braised Pork Sausages with Cabbage & Potatoes. A tight-fitting lid guarantees that Orange Cinnamon Rolls with Cream Cheese Icing emerge from the pot exquisitely soft. And Braised Chicken with Olives, Artichokes & Preserved Lemons showcases the pot's foolproof braising capabilities. Whichever recipe you choose, you'll be impressed with the dutch oven's ability to produce delicious meals with ease.

Cleaning and Care

To ensure the performance and durability of your dutch oven, follow these tips for cleaning and maintaining. If you take a few simple measures, your dutch oven could last for decades.

- Use silicone, wooden, or plastic cooking utensils with your dutch oven.

- When placing a hot dutch oven on your tabletop for serving, always set the pot on a wooden board, trivet, or silicone mat.

- Let the dutch oven cool down before washing it.

- Many dutch ovens can be washed in the dishwasher. However, washing by hand is recommended. Remove food residue with nylon or soft abrasive pads or brushes. To avoid damaging the enamel, do not use metallic pads or harsh, abrasive cleaning agents. Dry the pan thoroughly before storing it.

- Check the pot's handles and knobs regularly and retighten them as needed.

- Make sure your pot's knob is ovenproof if you plan to use it for roasting.

Carnitas with Pickled Red Onion

In Mexico, this street-food favorite is prepared by slowly simmering large pieces of pork in lard until the meat is fall-apart tender. Here, a Mexican lager replaces the lard with delicious, healthier results.

---

1 cup red wine vinegar

1 teaspoon sugar

Kosher salt and freshly ground pepper

1 red onion, thinly sliced

1 boneless pork shoulder roast (3–4 lb)

¼ cup canola oil

1 yellow onion, finely chopped

2 cloves garlic, minced

1 bottle (12 fl oz) Mexican lager–style beer

2 cans (4 oz each) diced green peppers, with liquid

¼ teaspoon ground cinnamon

1 chipotle chile in adobo sauce

2 cups chicken broth

Juice of 1 large orange

Warm corn or flour tortillas, lime wedges, salsa, and chopped cilantro, for serving

In a 5-qt dutch oven over medium-high heat, combine the vinegar, sugar, and 1 teaspoon salt and stir until the sugar and salt have dissolved. Place the red onion in a bowl and pour the vinegar mixture over it. Let cool to room temperature, then refrigerate for up to 1 week until ready to use. Wipe out the pot with a paper towel.

Preheat the oven to 350°F.

Season the pork roast with salt and pepper. Place the pot over medium-high heat and warm the oil. Cook the pork until browned, about 2 minutes per side. Transfer to a platter.

Pour off all but a thin layer of the fat from the pot and place over medium-high heat. Add the yellow onion and garlic and cook, stirring occasionally, until they begin to soften, 1–2 minutes. Add the beer, stirring to scrape up the browned bits. Add the green peppers with their liquid, cinnamon, and chipotle chile and stir well to combine.

Return the pork to the pot, add the broth and orange juice, and bring to a simmer. Cover, transfer to the oven, and cook until the pork is tender, 3–3½ hours. Transfer the pork to a cutting board and cover loosely with aluminum foil until ready to carve. Skim the fat off the cooking liquid. Using a sharp knife and a fork, cut and shred the pork into bite-size pieces. Arrange the meat on a platter and moisten it lightly with the cooking liquid. Serve right away with the pickled red onion, tortillas, lime wedges, salsa, and cilantro.

SERVES 6–8

CARNITAS IS PERFECT for a party. Cook the meat the night before and let cool, then refrigerate overnight. Reheat and shred before serving.

AFTER PICKING THE CILANTRO leaves for the garnish, tie the stems together with kitchen twine. Add to the dutch oven while braising the chicken, then remove before serving.

Coconut-Braised Chicken Thighs with Lemongrass

The flavorful meat of chicken thighs is ideal for this aromatic Southeast Asian–style braise. Higher in fat and collagen than breasts, thighs are less likely to toughen during a long, slow simmer. An equal amount of baby spinach or baby mustard greens can replace the kale.

Preheat the oven to 375°F.

Pat the chicken dry and season generously with salt and pepper. In a 5-qt dutch oven over medium-high heat, warm the oil. Working in batches, add the chicken and cook until golden brown on both sides, about 3 minutes per side. Transfer to a plate. Pour off all but 1 tablespoon of the fat from the pot.

Place the pot over medium heat, add the green onions, lemongrass, and chile, and cook, stirring occasionally, until tender, about 4 minutes.

Return the chicken to the pot. Add the coconut milk, potatoes, garlic, cinnamon, coriander, star anise, and lemon wedges and bring to a simmer. Cover, transfer to the oven, and cook until the chicken is cooked through and the potatoes can be easily pierced with a knife, 30–45 minutes.

Remove the pot from the oven, discard the star anise, and stir in the lime juice. Add the kale and stir until just wilted. Adjust the seasoning with salt and pepper.

Serve over steamed rice, and garnish with cilantro.

SERVES 4

2½ lb boneless chicken thighs

Kosher salt and freshly ground pepper

1 tablespoon olive oil

2 green onions, white and pale green parts, chopped

2 lemongrass stalks, white part only, thinly sliced

2 tablespoons minced serrano chile

2 cans (13.5 fl oz each) coconut milk

1 lb Yukon gold potatoes, peeled and cut into 2-inch pieces

6–8 cloves garlic, peeled and smashed

2 teaspoons *each* ground cinnamon and ground coriander

1 star anise

1 large lemon, cut into 8 wedges

Juice of 1 lime

3 cups baby kale

Steamed rice, for serving

Chopped fresh cilantro, for garnish

Asparagus & Pea Risotto with Parmesan & Mint

Put this lovely risotto on the menu in spring, when asparagus and peas are in the market. Always select a good-quality broth for risotto. Because it is added to the rice in small amounts throughout the cooking process, its flavor infuses the kernels.

Kosher salt and freshly ground pepper

1 lb asparagus, ends trimmed, spears cut on the bias into 1-inch pieces

2 tablespoons olive oil

2 shallots, minced

2 cloves garlic, minced

1½ cups Arborio rice

½ cup dry white wine

6 cups chicken or vegetable broth, warmed

¼ cup crème fraîche

½ cup fresh shelled or frozen peas

¼ cup grated Parmesan cheese

2 tablespoons chopped fresh mint

Toasted pine nuts, for garnish (optional)

Fill a 5-qt dutch oven with salted water and bring to a boil over medium-high heat. Add the asparagus and cook until tender-crisp, about 3 minutes. Drain and set aside. Dry the pot.

Place the pot over medium heat and warm the oil. Add the shallots and cook, stirring occasionally, until translucent, about 3 minutes. Add the garlic and cook, stirring occasionally, for 1 minute. Add the rice and cook, stirring occasionally, until toasted, about 3 minutes. Add the wine and stir until it is absorbed. Add 2 cups of the broth and cook, stirring constantly, until it is almost completely absorbed, about 10 minutes. Reduce heat to low and continue adding broth ½ cup at a time, stirring constantly until it is almost completely absorbed before adding more.

When the rice is tender and the risotto is creamy, after about 30 minutes, stir in half of the crème fraîche until blended. Stir in the peas, asparagus, Parmesan, and mint, and season with salt and pepper. Add more broth if needed to reach the desired consistency.

Divide the risotto among shallow bowls and top with the remaining crème fraîche and pine nuts (if using). Serve right away.

SERVES 4–6

THE KEY TO PERFECT risotto is cooking it slowly over low heat. Your patience will be rewarded with a delicious dish!

FOR A LIGHTER TAKE,
sub ground turkey for the beef,
or omit the meat and let the
sweet potatoes and beans
do the heavy lifting.

Game-Day Chili

You can make this chili the day before the big game and then reheat it just before kickoff. Set out the garnishes so diners can customize their own bowls, and bake a big batch of corn bread for mopping up every delicious drop.

In a 5-qt dutch oven over medium heat, warm the oil. Add the onion and cook, stirring occasionally, until tender and translucent, about 4 minutes. Add the ground beef, garlic, chili powder, and cumin and cook, breaking up the meat with a wooden spoon, until browned, about 5 minutes. Spoon off any excess fat.

Add the sweet potatoes, tequila (if using), black beans, tomatoes with their juices, chipotle chiles and adobo sauce, and broth and bring to a simmer. Reduce the heat to medium-low, cover, and cook until the sweet potatoes are tender, about 35 minutes. Uncover and cook until the chili is slightly thickened, 5–10 minutes longer. Season with salt and pepper.

Ladle the chili into bowls and top with avocado, sour cream, tortilla chips, and cheese. Serve right away.

SERVES 6–8

1 tablespoon olive oil

1 yellow onion, diced

1 lb lean ground beef

2 cloves garlic, minced

1 teaspoon chili powder

1 teaspoon ground cumin

2 sweet potatoes, peeled and cut into ½-inch dice

¼ cup tequila (optional)

1 can (15 oz) black beans, drained and rinsed

1 can (28 oz) diced tomatoes

2 chipotle chiles in adobo sauce, minced, plus 1 tablespoon adobo sauce

2 cups vegetable broth

Kosher salt and freshly ground pepper

Sliced avocado, sour cream, crushed tortilla chips, and grated Cheddar cheese, for garnish

Curried Meatballs with Spicy Tomato Sauce

After mixing the meatballs, fry a small bit of the meat until cooked through and taste for seasoning. These meatballs are very tender and delicate, but if they are not holding their shape, add up to ½ cup dried bread crumbs to the mixture.

For the meatballs

2 tablespoons olive oil

1 yellow onion, minced

3 cloves garlic, minced

2-inch piece fresh ginger, peeled and minced

2 lb lean ground beef

2 teaspoons garam masala

1 teaspoon ground cumin

1 teaspoon ground coriander

½ teaspoon cayenne pepper

Kosher salt

½ cup fresh cilantro, minced

Juice of 1 lemon

1 large egg, lightly beaten

¼ cup plain whole-milk yogurt

To make the meatballs, in a 5-qt dutch oven over medium-high heat, warm 1 tablespoon of the oil. Add the onion and cook, stirring occasionally, until tender and translucent, about 4 minutes. Add the garlic and ginger and cook, stirring occasionally, until fragrant, about 1 minute. Transfer the onion mixture to a large bowl and let cool completely. Add the ground beef, garam masala, cumin, coriander, cayenne, 1 teaspoon salt, the cilantro, lemon juice, egg, and yogurt to the bowl. Mix gently with your hands until the ingredients are incorporated and the mixture starts to become sticky. Using a spoon or a 2-oz ice cream scoop, form the mixture into golf ball–size meatballs and place on a baking sheet.

Wipe out the pot with a paper towel. Place over medium-high heat and warm the remaining 1 tablespoon oil. Working in batches, sear the meatballs on all sides until nicely browned, about 2 minutes per side. Transfer to a plate.

To make the sauce, let the pot cool and wipe it out with a paper towel. Place over medium-high heat and warm the oil. Add the onion and cook, stirring occasionally, until slightly caramelized, about 8 minutes. Add the garlic, ginger, cumin, coriander, curry powder, garam masala, cayenne, and 1 teaspoon salt and cook, stirring occasionally, until fragrant, about 1 minute. Stir in the tomatoes and ½ cup water and bring to a simmer. Adjust the seasoning with salt and black pepper.

Gently nestle the meatballs in the sauce and bring to a simmer. Cover and cook until the meatballs are cooked through, about 15 minutes.

Serve the meatballs over steamed rice, and garnish with cilantro and green onions.

SERVES 4–6

For the sauce

1 tablespoon olive oil

1 yellow onion, chopped

2 cloves garlic, minced

2-inch piece fresh ginger, peeled and minced

2 teaspoons ground cumin

2 teaspoons ground coriander

1 teaspoon curry powder

1 teaspoon garam masala

½ teaspoon cayenne pepper

Kosher salt and freshly ground black pepper

1 can (28 oz) crushed tomatoes

Steamed jasmine or basmati rice, for serving

Fresh cilantro leaves and sliced green onions, for garnish

Faux Chicken Pho

A dutch oven makes an ideal soup pot. Its thick walls and base provide the steady, even heat needed for maintaining the uniform simmer most soups require, including this easy-to-assemble riff on a staple of the Vietnamese table.

2 tablespoons olive oil

1 yellow onion, minced

2 cloves garlic, minced

½ lb shiitake mushrooms, brushed clean, stemmed, and thinly sliced

1 star anise

1 cinnamon stick or ¼ teaspoon ground cinnamon

Pinch of red pepper flakes

2 skin-on, bone-in chicken breasts (about 1½ lb total)

6 cups chicken broth

½-inch piece peeled fresh ginger, sliced into thin rounds

Kosher salt

2 teaspoons Asian fish sauce

1 package (8 oz) rice noodles, softened in hot water and drained

Sliced green onions, sliced jalapeño chile, fresh mint leaves, and lime wedges, for serving

In a 5-qt dutch oven over medium-high heat, warm the oil. Add the onion and cook, stirring occasionally, until translucent, about 3 minutes. Add the garlic and mushrooms and cook, stirring occasionally, until the mushrooms are tender, about 3 minutes. Add the star anise, cinnamon, and red pepper flakes and cook, stirring occasionally, for 30 seconds. Add the chicken, broth, ginger, and a pinch of salt and bring to a boil. Reduce the heat to medium-low and simmer until the chicken is cooked through, about 25 minutes.

Using tongs, transfer the chicken to a plate. When it's cool enough to handle, remove the meat, discarding the skin and bones, and tear into bite-size pieces.

Add the chicken, fish sauce, and rice noodles to the pot and stir to combine. Serve right away with green onions, jalapeño, mint leaves, and lime wedges alongside.

SERVES 4

FOR A LIGHTER MEAL,
replace the rice noodles
with spiralized vegetables.

ALLOW THE CHICKEN to soak in the buttermilk marinade overnight for an extra-tender bite under the perfectly crispy skin.

Buttermilk Fried Chicken

Southern cooks traditionally give chicken pieces a buttermilk bath before frying, knowing that the acids and enzymes in the buttermilk will help tenderize the meat. Accompany this spicy classic with cooling coleslaw, mashed potatoes, and warm buttermilk biscuits.

Place the chicken pieces on a baking sheet. In a large bowl, stir together 4 cups of the flour, 1 tablespoon salt, and 1 tablespoon black pepper. Toss the chicken to lightly coat with the flour mixture. In another large bowl, stir together the buttermilk, 1 tablespoon salt, 1 tablespoon black pepper, 1 tablespoon of the cayenne, and the Tabasco. Place the chicken in the buttermilk mixture and turn until coated. Cover and refrigerate for at least 30 minutes or up to overnight.

Remove the chicken from the refrigerator 15 minutes before frying. Preheat the oven to 350°F. Place a wire cooling rack on a baking sheet. Fill a 5-qt dutch oven two-thirds full with oil and heat over high heat until it reaches 350°F on a deep-frying thermometer; adjust the heat to keep the oil at 340°–360°F.

In a large bowl, stir together the remaining 4 cups flour and 1 tablespoon cayenne, 1 tablespoon salt, 1 tablespoon black pepper, and the baking powder. Remove the chicken from the buttermilk mixture and toss to coat with the flour mixture. Working in batches, use tongs to carefully place the chicken in the hot oil, stirring if the pieces stick to each other. Fry, turning once, until deep golden brown, 10–15 minutes. Transfer the chicken to the prepared cooling rack. Check the internal temperature of the chicken with an instant-read thermometer; if less than 165°F, roast the chicken in the oven for 10–15 minutes. Serve warm or cold.

SERVES 4–6

8 skin-on, bone-in chicken pieces (wings, thighs, drumsticks, breasts) (about 3½ lb total)

8 cups all-purpose flour

Kosher salt and freshly ground black pepper

4 cups buttermilk

2 tablespoons cayenne pepper

1 tablespoon Tabasco or other hot sauce

8–12 cups canola oil

1½ teaspoons baking powder

Mussels with Fennel & White Wine

If you buy the mussels a day in advance, place them in a shallow bowl, cover them with a damp cloth, and store the bowl on the lowest shelf in the refrigerator. For an interesting shellfish mix, use half mussels and half littleneck clams.

For the garlic butter

4 tablespoons unsalted butter, at room temperature

4 cloves garlic, minced

Kosher salt

2 tablespoons unsalted butter

2 tablespoons olive oil

4 shallots, thinly sliced

2 fennel bulbs, trimmed, cored, and thinly sliced

4 cloves garlic, minced

1 cup white wine

1 can (28 oz) diced tomatoes

½ teaspoon saffron threads (optional)

Kosher salt and freshly ground pepper

3 lb mussels, scrubbed and debearded

1 tablespoon chopped fresh flat-leaf parsley

1 tablespoon chopped fresh tarragon

Toasted crusty bread slices, for serving

To make the garlic butter, in a small bowl, stir together the butter, garlic, and ½ teaspoon salt. Set aside.

In a 5-qt dutch oven over medium heat, melt the butter with the oil. Add the shallots and fennel and cook, stirring occasionally, until tender, about 5 minutes. Add the garlic and cook, stirring occasionally, until fragrant, about 1 minute. Add the wine and simmer until slightly reduced, about 3 minutes. Add the tomatoes and their juices, crumble in the saffron (if using), add 1 teaspoon salt, and 1 teaspoon pepper, and stir to combine. Simmer for 5 minutes, then increase the heat to high and bring to a boil. Add the mussels, reduce the heat to medium, cover, and cook until the mussels open, 6–8 minutes. Discard any mussels that did not open. Stir in the parsley and tarragon.

Stir 1 tablespoon of the garlic butter into the broth. Spread the remaining garlic butter on the toasted bread slices. Divide the mussels and broth among bowls and serve with the bread for dipping.

SERVES 4–6

Bouillabaisse

A classic of coastal Provence, this fish stew typically includes a heady mix of fennel seeds and saffron in the cooking liquid that flavors a generous measure of fish and shellfish. Serve it with rouille (spicy, garlicky saffron mayonnaise) and toasted baguette slices.

2 tablespoons olive oil

1 large yellow onion, chopped

4 cloves garlic, thinly sliced

½ teaspoon saffron threads

1 teaspoon fennel seeds

1 teaspoon chopped fresh thyme

1 teaspoon chopped fresh oregano

½ teaspoon smoked paprika

Large pinch of red pepper flakes

1 can (28 oz) diced tomatoes

4 cups fish or chicken broth

Kosher salt and freshly ground black pepper

1 lb cod, ling cod, rockfish, halibut, or other lean white-fleshed fish fillets, cut into bite-size pieces

1 lb assorted seafood, such as peeled and deveined large shrimp, clams, and/or mussels, scrubbed and debearded

In a 5-qt dutch oven over medium-low heat, warm the oil. Add the onion and garlic and cook, stirring occasionally, until the onion is soft but not browned, about 5 minutes. Crumble in the saffron and add the fennel seeds, thyme, oregano, paprika, and red pepper flakes. Cook, stirring occasionally, for 1 minute. Add the tomatoes with their juices, broth, and ¼ teaspoon salt, increase the heat to medium-high, and bring to a boil. Reduce the heat to low and simmer until the liquid is slightly reduced, about 30 minutes.

Add the fish and seafood, increase the heat to medium-low, and cook until the shrimp are opaque throughout, the clams and mussels open, and the fish begins to flake apart, 6–8 minutes. Discard any clams and mussels that did not open. Adjust the seasoning with salt and black pepper. Ladle the stew into bowls and serve right away.

SERVES 4–6

Five-Spice Beef Stew with Green Beans

If desired, thinly slice the dark green tops of the green onions and use as a garnish. You can find five-spice powder in most well-stocked grocery stores and Asian markets. If not, add a pinch each of ground cloves, cinnamon, Sichuan peppers, and fennel seeds.

Preheat the oven to 375°F.

Season the beef generously with salt and black pepper. In a 5-qt dutch oven over medium-high heat, warm 1 tablespoon of the oil. Working in batches, add the beef and sear until browned on all sides, about 3 minutes per side. Transfer to a plate.

Let the pot cool slightly, then warm the remaining 1 tablespoon oil over medium heat. Add the garlic, ginger, shallot, and green onions and cook, stirring occasionally, until fragrant, about 1 minute. Add the five-spice powder, red pepper flakes, star anise (if using), brown sugar, wine, and soy sauce and cook, stirring occasionally, until slightly reduced, about 2 minutes.

Return the beef to the pot, add the broth, increase the heat to high, and bring to a boil. Cover, transfer to the oven, and cook until the meat is very tender, 2½–3 hours. Stir in the green beans and return the uncovered pot to the oven. Cook until the beans are tender, about 10 minutes. Adjust the seasoning with salt and black pepper or more soy sauce.

Ladle the stew over steamed rice and serve right away.

SERVES 4–6

---

3 lb boneless beef stew meat, cut into 2-inch chunks

Kosher salt and freshly ground black pepper

2 tablespoons vegetable oil

4 cloves garlic, minced

2-inch piece fresh ginger, peeled and grated

1 shallot, thinly sliced

4 green onions, white and pale green parts, thinly sliced

1½ teaspoons Chinese five-spice powder

½ teaspoon red pepper flakes

1 star anise (optional)

2 teaspoons firmly packed light brown sugar

3 tablespoons Chinese rice wine or dry sherry

3 tablespoons soy sauce, plus more as needed

4 cups vegetable or beef broth

½ lb green beans, trimmed and halved crosswise

Steamed rice, for serving

GNOCCHI ARE SMALL ITALIAN dumplings traditionally made from potatoes and can be found with the pasta in the grocery store.

Gnocchi with Beef Ragù

A heavy pot, a steady low temperature, and a long simmer will produce the best ragù. Here, the addition of a little butter at the end of cooking gives the sauce a decadent finish. This ragù is also excellent tossed with pappardelle or rigatoni.

In a 5-qt dutch oven over medium-high heat, warm the oil. Add the bacon and ground beef and cook, breaking up the meat with a wooden spoon, until the meat is cooked through and browned bits stick to the bottom of the pot, 8–10 minutes. Using a slotted spoon, transfer the meat to a bowl. Pour off all but about 3 tablespoons of the fat from the pot.

Place the pot over medium heat, add the onion, garlic, bay leaf, and red pepper flakes, and cook, stirring occasionally, until the onion is translucent, about 4 minutes. Add the tomato paste and stir well. Add the tomatoes and wine, increase the heat to medium-high, and bring to a simmer. Add the broth and bring to a gentle simmer.

Return the meat to the pot, reduce the heat to medium-low, and simmer gently until the sauce is reduced and richly flavored, about 30 minutes. Stir in the butter and season with salt and black pepper.

Meanwhile, cook the gnocchi according to the package instructions.

Spoon the ragù over the gnocchi and garnish with basil leaves, if using. Sprinkle with Parmesan and serve right away.

SERVES 4–6

2 tablespoons olive oil

3 oz bacon, finely chopped

2 lb lean ground beef

1 yellow onion, diced

2 cloves garlic, minced

1 bay leaf

½ teaspoon red pepper flakes

2 tablespoons tomato paste

1 can (28 oz) crushed tomatoes

¾ cup red wine

3 cups chicken broth

2 tablespoons unsalted butter

Kosher salt and freshly ground black pepper

1 lb gnocchi

Basil leaves, for garnish (optional)

Grated Parmesan cheese, for serving

Pork Belly Ramen

This rich, satisfying soup develops its intense flavor from oven-braising the pork belly in a complex liquid that becomes part of the broth. Select a slab of pork from the center of the belly, which has even layers of fat and meat.

8 dried shiitake mushrooms

1 cup hot water

3 tablespoons canola oil

1 lb skin-on center-cut pork belly

1 yellow onion, diced

1 head garlic, cloves peeled and left whole

1-inch piece fresh ginger, peeled and chopped

⅓ cup rice vinegar

2 tablespoons soy sauce

2 tablespoons mirin

Kosher salt

5 cups chicken broth

8 oz cooked ramen noodles

4–6 large eggs, hard-boiled for 5–6 minutes, peeled, and cut in half lengthwise

6 green onions, green parts only, finely sliced

Preheat the oven to 350°F.

Soak the dried mushrooms in the hot water for 20 minutes. Strain through a double layer of cheesecloth, reserving the liquid. Rinse the mushrooms in cold water and set aside.

In a 5-qt dutch oven over medium-high heat, warm the oil. Add the pork belly, skin side down, and cook until crispy, 3–4 minutes. Transfer to a plate.

Place the pot over medium-high heat, add the onion and garlic, and cook, stirring occasionally, until the onion is translucent, 6–8 minutes. Return the pork belly, skin side up, to the pot and add the mushrooms, soaking liquid, ginger, vinegar, soy sauce, mirin, and a large pinch of salt. Bring to a simmer, cover, transfer to the oven, and cook until the pork belly is fork-tender, about 2 hours. Transfer the pork belly to a cutting board. Using a slotted spoon, transfer the mushrooms to a small bowl. Thinly slice the pork and set aside.

Transfer the braising liquid to a blender or food processor and blend until smooth. Add the broth and blend again. Return the broth mixture to the pot and adjust the seasoning with salt. Keep warm over low heat.

Divide the noodles among the bowls and ladle the broth on top. Add slices of pork belly, mushrooms, egg halves, and green onions and serve.

SERVES 4–6

BRAISE THE PORK BELLY
ahead of time and refrigerate,
then reheat before assembling
the ramen bowls.

IF YOU CAN'T FIND
grits at your supermarket,
substitute polenta.

Shrimp & Grits

This homey dish was born in the Lowcountry of South Carolina and Georgia, where it is traditionally eaten for breakfast, but it has since spread to other locales and mealtimes. Here, cleanup is minimal because a single pot is used for cooking both the grits and the shrimp.

In a 5-qt dutch oven over high heat, bring 4½ cups water to a boil. Gradually whisk in the grits, then reduce the heat to low and dot the grits with the butter. Simmer, stirring frequently, until the grits are very soft and thickened, about 30 minutes, adding more water if the mixture becomes too dry. Fold in the crème fraîche. Transfer the grits to a bowl and cover with aluminum foil. Wipe out the pot with a paper towel.

Place the pot over medium heat and warm the oil. Add the sausage (if using), bell pepper, onion, and garlic and cook, stirring occasionally, until the vegetables are tender, about 8 minutes. Add the shrimp, tomatoes with their juices, and Old Bay seasoning and cook, stirring occasionally, until the shrimp are opaque throughout, about 6 minutes. Season with salt and pepper.

Divide the grits among the bowls, spoon the shrimp mixture on top, garnish with parsley, and serve right away.

SERVES 4–6

1 cup grits or polenta (not instant)

4 tablespoons unsalted butter, thinly sliced

¼ cup crème fraîche

¼ cup olive oil

½ lb smoked andouille sausage, thinly sliced (optional)

1 red bell pepper, seeded and thinly sliced

1 yellow onion, diced

4 cloves garlic, minced

1 lb large shrimp, peeled and deveined

1 can (15 oz) diced tomatoes

2 teaspoons Old Bay or other seafood seasoning

Kosher salt and freshly ground pepper

Chopped fresh flat-leaf parsley, for garnish

Moroccan Chickpea & Lentil Stew

This stew freezes well for up to one month. Expect a thicker, chunkier stew if you use red lentils, which break down when cooked. Spoon this boldly flavored dish over steamed rice or couscous.

---

3 tablespoons olive oil

1 yellow onion, thinly sliced

2 ribs celery, thinly sliced

2 cloves garlic, minced

1 teaspoon ground ginger

½ teaspoon *each* ground turmeric, nutmeg, and cinnamon

Kosher salt and freshly ground pepper

1½ cups green or red lentils

6 cups vegetable broth or water

1 can (28 oz) crushed tomatoes

1 can (15 oz) chickpeas, drained and rinsed

2 teaspoons fresh lemon juice

For the yogurt sauce

½ cup Greek yogurt

Zest of 1 lemon

For the cilantro pesto

½ cup fresh cilantro leaves, roughly chopped

Juice of 1 lemon

¼ cup olive oil

Toasted sliced almonds, for serving

In a 5-qt dutch oven over medium heat, warm the oil. Add the onion and cook, stirring occasionally, until tender and slightly caramelized, about 8 minutes. Add the celery and cook, stirring occasionally, until tender, about 3 minutes. Add the garlic, ginger, turmeric, nutmeg, cinnamon, 1½ teaspoons salt, and ¼ teaspoon pepper and cook, stirring occasionally, until fragrant, about 1 minute.

Add the lentils, broth, and tomatoes and stir to combine. Increase the heat to medium-high, bring to a boil, then reduce the heat to medium-low and gently simmer until the lentils are tender, 30–35 minutes. Add the chickpeas and cook until warmed through, about 5 minutes.

Meanwhile, make the yogurt sauce: In a small bowl, stir together the yogurt and lemon zest, and season with salt and pepper.

To make the cilantro pesto, in a mini food processor, combine the cilantro and lemon juice and pulse until well blended. With the processor running, add the oil in a slow, steady stream until the mixture is smooth. Season with salt and pepper.

Serve the stew warm with the yogurt sauce, cilantro pesto, and almonds.

SERVES 4–6

Tofu & Butternut Squash Curry

This easy Thai-style curry is the perfect go-to weeknight dish when the weather has turned cold. Trade out the butternut squash for kabocha, if you like, and for a vegetarian version, swap in tamari for the fish sauce.

Fill a 5-qt dutch oven with salted water and bring to a boil over medium-high heat. Add the green beans and cook until tender-crisp, about 3 minutes. Drain and set aside. Dry the pot.

In the same pot over medium-low heat, warm the oil. Add the onion and cook, stirring occasionally, until soft and translucent, 4–6 minutes. Add the garlic and ginger and cook, stirring occasionally, until fragrant, about 2 minutes. Add the squash, coconut milk, fish sauce, curry paste, lime juice, and sugar, increase heat to medium, and bring to a simmer. Cover partially and simmer until the squash is just tender, about 20 minutes. Add the bell peppers and cook until tender, about 2 minutes. Gently stir in the tofu and cook until warmed through, 2–3 minutes.

Spoon the curry over steamed rice, garnish with the basil, and serve right away.

SERVES 4–6

½ lb green beans, trimmed and halved

2 tablespoons vegetable oil

1 yellow onion, diced

2 cloves garlic, minced

3 tablespoons peeled and minced fresh ginger

1 butternut squash (about 1 lb), peeled, seeded, and cut into 1½-inch cubes

2 cans (13.5 fl oz each) coconut milk

¼ cup Asian fish sauce

3 tablespoons Thai red curry paste

2 tablespoons fresh lime juice

2 teaspoons sugar

2 red bell peppers, seeded and thinly sliced

1 package (14 oz) firm tofu, drained and cut into ¾-inch pieces

Steamed brown jasmine rice, for serving

⅓ cup slivered fresh basil

Whole-Roasted Cauliflower with Almond & Parsley Gremolata

Roasting a whole cauliflower in a hot oven caramelizes and concentrates its flavors and yields a moist, tender interior. Carry it whole to the table and slice it while your guests watch for a rave-worthy supper centerpiece.

---

1 head cauliflower

3 tablespoons olive oil plus ½ cup

Kosher salt and freshly ground black pepper

2 lemons, halved, plus lemon slices, for serving

For the gremolata

⅓ cup blanched, toasted unsalted almonds

2 cloves garlic

1 shallot, roughly chopped

½ cup fresh flat-leaf parsley leaves

3 tablespoons white balsamic vinegar

1 teaspoon honey

1 teaspoon Dijon mustard

Pinch of red pepper flakes

½ cup grated Parmesan cheese

¼ cup panko bread crumbs, toasted

Preheat the oven to 375°F.

Put the cauliflower in a 5-qt dutch oven. Drizzle with 2 tablespoons of the oil and season with salt and black pepper. Tuck the lemon halves around the cauliflower. Roast until the cauliflower is tender and golden brown, about 1 hour.

Meanwhile, make the gremolata. In a blender or food processor, combine the almonds, garlic, shallot, parsley, vinegar, honey, mustard, red pepper flakes, and the ½ cup oil and blend until smooth. Set the sauce aside.

In a small bowl, stir together the Parmesan, panko, and remaining 3 tablespoons oil.

Transfer the cauliflower to a cutting board, cut into thick wedges, and arrange on a platter. Drizzle with the sauce and sprinkle with the panko mixture. Serve warm with lemon slices alongside.

SERVES 4

MAKE THE GREMOLATA up to 2 days in advance and refrigerate, then bring to room temperature before serving.

CUSTOMIZE THIS LASAGNE
with other vegetables, such as
spinach, grilled bell peppers, or
roasted eggplant. To streamline
prep, swap the béchamel sauce
for store-bought tomato sauce.

Summer Vegetable Lasagne

Thanks to the tall, stout walls and uniform heat of a dutch oven, the layers of this vegetarian lasagne cook evenly and remain moist. Assemble in the morning, refrigerate, then slip into the oven an hour before dinner.

Preheat the oven to 375°F.

To make the vegetable filling, in a 5-qt dutch oven over medium heat, warm the oil. Add the onion and cook, stirring occasionally, until translucent, about 4 minutes. Add the mushrooms and squash and cook, stirring occasionally, until tender, about 7 minutes. Transfer to a bowl and let cool. Stir in the bell peppers, tomatoes, basil, and lemon zest, and season with salt and pepper. Set aside. Clean the pot.

To make the béchamel sauce, in the same pot over medium heat, melt the butter. Add the onion and cook, stirring occasionally, until softened, about 4 minutes. Add the flour and cook, stirring constantly, for 1 minute. Slowly stir in the milk and cook, stirring occasionally, until the sauce is thickened, about 4 minutes. Season with salt and pepper. Transfer half of the sauce to a bowl. Spread the remaining sauce evenly on the bottom of the pot. In another bowl, stir together the ricotta, egg, and a generous pinch each of salt and pepper.

Cover the sauce in the pot with a single layer of lasagne noodles, breaking them if needed to fit. Spread one-third of the ricotta mixture evenly on top, then one-third of the vegetable mixture. Sprinkle with one-fourth of the mozzarella. Repeat the layering 2 more times, starting with the noodles. Top with a final layer of noodles and the remaining béchamel sauce. Sprinkle with the remaining mozzarella. Cover the pot with aluminum foil and bake until the noodles are tender, about 45 minutes. Uncover and bake until the top is browned, about 15 minutes longer. Serve warm. Let rest for 15 minutes before serving.

SERVES 8–10

For the vegetable filling

1 tablespoon olive oil

½ yellow onion, finely diced

½ lb cremini mushrooms, brushed clean and chopped

2 yellow or green summer squash, cut into ½-inch dice

3 jarred roasted red bell peppers, roughly chopped

1 can (28 oz) plum tomatoes, drained and roughly chopped

1 cup fresh basil leaves, minced

Zest of 1 lemon

Kosher salt and freshly ground pepper

For the béchamel sauce

4 tablespoons unsalted butter

½ yellow onion, finely diced

¼ cup all-purpose flour

1½ cups whole milk

3 cups ricotta cheese

1 large egg, lightly beaten

½ lb no-boil lasagne noodles

¾ lb mozzarella cheese, shredded

Pasta & Cannellini Bean Soup

Once you have readied all of the ingredients for this quick-and-easy take on Italy's pasta e fagioli, the soup cooks for just a half hour. For a touch of color, add a few handfuls of baby spinach or chopped Swiss chard just before serving. Accompany with country-style bread.

1 tablespoon olive oil

¼ lb pancetta, diced

1 yellow onion, diced

Kosher salt and freshly ground black pepper

1 fresh rosemary sprig

1 fresh thyme sprig

1 bay leaf

3 cloves garlic, minced

1 teaspoon red pepper flakes

2 cans (15 oz each) cannellini beans, drained and rinsed

1 can (28 oz) diced tomatoes

1 tablespoon tomato paste

4 cups chicken broth

1½ cups ditalini or other small dried pasta

Chopped fresh flat-leaf parsley and grated Parmesan cheese, for garnish

In a 5-qt dutch oven over medium heat, warm the oil. Add the pancetta and cook, stirring frequently, until lightly browned, about 4 minutes. Add the onion, a pinch each of salt and black pepper, the rosemary, thyme, and bay leaf. Cook, stirring occasionally, until the onion is translucent, about 4 minutes. Stir in the garlic and red pepper flakes and cook, stirring occasionally, until fragrant, about 1 minute.

Add the cannellini beans, tomatoes with their juices, tomato paste, broth, and 2 cups water and simmer for 15 minutes to allow the flavors to meld. Increase the heat to high and bring to a rapid boil, then add the pasta. Cook, stirring occasionally, until the pasta is al dente (tender but firm to the bite), 6–8 minutes or according to the package instructions. Remove and discard the herb stems and bay leaf. Adjust the seasoning with salt and black pepper.

Ladle the soup into bowls and garnish with parsley and Parmesan.

SERVES 4–6

Cider-Braised Pork Sausages with Cabbage & Potatoes

Because a good-quality dutch oven conducts and holds heat well, this German-inspired meal-in-a-pot will cook slowly and evenly, ensuring the flavors mellow and blend. Pour a German pilsner or bock beer at the table. You can substitute chicken apple sausages for the bratwurst if desired.

In a 5-qt dutch oven over medium heat, warm the oil. Add the onions and cook, stirring occasionally, until very soft and golden brown, about 10 minutes.

Stir in the cabbage, apple, potatoes, caraway seeds, cider, vinegar, brown sugar, 1 tablespoon salt, and 1 teaspoon pepper. Cover and cook, stirring occasionally, until the cabbage is very soft, about 1 hour.

Tuck the sausages into the cabbage mixture, cover, and cook until the sausages are heated through, about 20 minutes. Serve warm with mustard.

SERVES 4–6

2 tablespoons olive oil

2 yellow onions, thinly sliced

1 large head green cabbage (about 3 lb), cored and thinly sliced

1 large tart green apple, such as Granny Smith, peeled, cored, and chopped

1 lb Yukon gold potatoes, quartered

2 teaspoons caraway seeds

1 cup apple cider

⅓ cup cider vinegar

2 tablespoons firmly packed light brown sugar

Kosher salt and freshly ground pepper

2 lb precooked pork sausages, such as bratwurst

Whole-grain mustard, for serving

Maple-Bourbon Short Ribs

Tasting of smoke and caramel, bourbon, America's national whiskey, contributes big flavor to this comfort-food staple. To get a rich brown sear on the ribs, pat them dry before seasoning them and then make sure the oil is hot before you slide them into the pot.

3 lb boneless beef short ribs

Kosher salt and freshly ground pepper

2 tablespoons olive oil

1 yellow onion, diced

4 cloves garlic, minced

¾ cup bourbon

½ cup maple syrup

2½ cups vegetable or beef broth, plus more as needed

1 tablespoon minced fresh rosemary

2 tablespoons tomato paste

1 tablespoon Worcestershire sauce

For the glaze

⅔ cup maple syrup

2 tablespoons Worcestershire sauce

Kosher salt and freshly ground pepper

Mashed sweet potatoes, for serving

Preheat the oven to 325°F.

Season the short ribs generously with salt and pepper. In a 5-qt dutch oven over medium-high heat, warm 1 tablespoon of the oil. Working in batches, add the short ribs and sear until browned on all sides, about 3 minutes per side. Transfer to a plate.

Let the pot cool slightly, then warm the remaining 1 tablespoon oil over medium heat. Add the onion and cook, stirring occasionally, until slightly caramelized, about 8 minutes. Add the garlic and cook, stirring occasionally, until fragrant, about 1 minute. Add the bourbon and maple syrup and cook until reduced by half, about 3 minutes. Stir in the broth, rosemary, tomato paste, and Worcestershire sauce. Nestle the short ribs in the sauce so they are almost completely covered with liquid, adding more broth or water if needed. Increase the heat to medium-high and bring to a boil. Cover, transfer to the oven, and cook, stirring every 45 minutes, until the ribs are very tender, 2–2½ hours. Transfer the ribs to a serving platter and cover loosely with aluminum foil.

Meanwhile, make the glaze. In a small saucepan over high heat, combine the maple syrup and Worcestershire sauce and bring to a boil. Cook, stirring, until reduced to a thick glaze, about 5 minutes. Season with salt and pepper.

Place the short ribs on top of the mashed sweet potatoes, drizzle the glaze over the ribs, and serve right away.

SERVES 4–6

YOU CAN SKIP THE GLAZE and instead let the braising liquid stand for 5 minutes, then skim off the fat. Boil the liquid over high heat until reduced to a thick sauce, about 10 minutes. Season with salt and pepper and return the short ribs to the sauce before serving.

PRESERVED LEMON
is sold in most specialty grocery
stores. If you can't find it,
substitute a squeeze of fresh
lemon juice and a pinch of salt.

Braised Chicken with Olives, Artichokes & Preserved Lemon

Serve this Moroccan-inspired dish with sliced cucumbers, tomatoes, and warm flatbread on the side. Browning the chicken before braising adds both flavor and color.

Fill a large bowl with water and add the juice of ½ lemon. Trim the stem of each artichoke. Snap off the outer leaves until you reach the tender inner leaves. Cut off the top one-third of the artichoke. Halve the artichokes lengthwise and cut each half in half. Add the artichokes to the lemon water.

Preheat the oven to 350°F.

Season the chicken with salt and black pepper. In a 5-qt dutch oven over medium-high heat, warm the oil. Working in batches, add the chicken and cook until browned on both sides, 8–10 minutes per batch. Transfer to a plate. Pour off some of the fat from the pot. Place the pot over medium heat, add the garlic, shallots, rosemary, fennel seeds, and red pepper flakes and cook, stirring occasionally, until fragrant, about 2 minutes. Add the wine and cook, stirring to scrape up the browned bits, until slightly reduced, about 2 minutes. Add the broth, lemon zest, lemon slices, and a big pinch each of salt and black pepper.

Bring the liquid to a simmer, and return the chicken to the pot. Cover, transfer to the oven, and cook for 45 minutes. Remove from the oven, nestle the artichoke hearts in the pot, and cook until the chicken is cooked through and the artichokes are tender, 35–45 minutes longer.

Using a slotted spoon, transfer the chicken and artichokes to a bowl and cover with aluminum foil. Place the pot over medium heat and simmer until the sauce is reduced by half, 6–8 minutes. Stir in the olives and preserved lemon. Adjust the seasoning with salt and pepper. Return the chicken and artichokes to the pot, garnish with the parsley, and serve.

SERVES 4–6

2 lemons, cut into slices

4 baby artichokes

8 skin-on, bone-in chicken thighs (about 3½ lb total)

Kosher salt and freshly ground black pepper

¼ cup olive oil

6 cloves garlic, minced

3 shallots, minced

1 tablespoon roughly chopped fresh rosemary

½ teaspoon crushed fennel seeds

½ teaspoon red pepper flakes

⅓ cup dry white wine

1 cup chicken broth

1½ teaspoons grated lemon zest

1 cup black and green unpitted olives (about 1 lb)

2 tablespoons rinsed and chopped preserved lemon

3 tablespoons chopped fresh flat-leaf parsley

Garlic Chicken Braised with Tarragon & Vermouth

A pot with a tight-fitting lid is indispensable for braises such as this one, where loss of moisture through evaporation will rob the finished dish of its prized succulence. Serve the chicken over steamed rice or buttered noodles for soaking up the garlicky sauce.

1 chicken (3–4 lb), cut into 10 pieces

Kosher salt and freshly ground pepper

¼ cup olive oil

1 yellow onion, diced

4 ribs celery, diced

2 heads garlic, cloves peeled and left whole

1 tablespoon chopped fresh tarragon, plus more for garnish

½ cup vermouth or dry white wine

1 cup chicken broth

Preheat the oven to 350°F.

Season the chicken generously with salt and pepper. In a 5-qt dutch oven over medium-high heat, warm the oil. Working in batches, add the chicken and cook until browned on both sides, 8–10 minutes per batch. Transfer to a plate. Pour off half the fat from the pot.

Place the pot over medium-high heat, add the onion and celery, and cook, stirring occasionally, until soft, 6–8 minutes. Add the garlic, tarragon, and a large pinch each of salt and pepper. Add the vermouth, stirring to scrape up the browned bits. Increase the heat to high and cook for 1 minute.

Return the chicken to the pot, add the broth, and bring to a simmer. Cover, transfer to the oven, and cook until the chicken is tender and cooked through, 1–1½ hours.

Serve the chicken and sauce right away, garnished with tarragon.

SERVES 4–6

Easy Overnight Bread

Here, a dutch oven mimics the covered clay pot traditionally favored by some European bakers for the beautifully browned crust it delivers. The moisture in the dough that would escape in a typical bread pan instead becomes steam that helps to crisp and color the exterior.

½ teaspoon instant yeast

Kosher salt

1½ cups lukewarm (110°–120°F) water

3 cups all-purpose flour, plus more for dusting

In a large bowl, stir together the yeast, 1½ teaspoons salt, the water, and about ½ cup of the flour. Let stand until the yeast starts to bubble, about 5 minutes. Add the remaining flour and stir until a shaggy, sticky dough forms. Cover the bowl with plastic wrap and let the dough rise at room temperature for 12–18 hours until doubled in bulk.

Punch down the dough, turn it out onto a lightly floured work surface, and shape into a ball. Cover with plastic wrap or a kitchen towel and let rise until doubled in bulk, 1–2 hours. About 30 minutes before the dough is ready, preheat the oven to 450°F and place a 5-qt dutch oven inside as the oven preheats.

Uncover the dough and knead until smooth and slightly elastic, about 3 minutes, then shape into a tight ball. Cover with plastic wrap and let stand for 15 minutes. Carefully remove the pot from the hot oven and place the dough, seam side down, in the pot. Cover and bake for 30 minutes. Uncover the pot and bake until the bread is golden brown, 10–15 minutes longer. Let the bread cool in the pot on a wire rack for at least 20 minutes before serving.

MAKES 1 SMALL LOAF

MAKE THE DOUGH
the evening before and proof
overnight in the refrigerator.
Let stand at room temperature
for 30 minutes, then roll out.

Orange Cinnamon Rolls with Cream Cheese Icing

Baking these rolls in a tightly covered Dutch oven ensures they will be wonderfully soft on the inside and golden on the outside. For a flavorful crunch, add ½ cup chopped pecans with the orange zest.

In the bowl of a stand mixer fitted with the dough hook, stir together the milk and yeast and let stand until the yeast starts to bubble, about 5 minutes. Add the egg, 2 tablespoons of the butter, flour, ¼ cup of the brown sugar, and 1 teaspoon salt and beat on medium speed until the dough comes together and is smooth, 3–4 minutes. Transfer the dough to a lightly oiled bowl and turn to coat all sides. Cover with plastic wrap and let the dough rise at room temperature until almost doubled in bulk, about 1 hour.

Meanwhile, in a small bowl, stir together the remaining ½ cup brown sugar, the cinnamon, orange zest, and a pinch of salt. Set aside.

Punch down the dough and turn it out onto a lightly floured work surface. Roll out into a 14-by-12-inch rectangle. Spread the brown sugar mixture over the dough all the way to the edges. Starting with a long end, roll the dough into a log and cut crosswise into 10–12 slices. Lightly grease a 5-qt dutch oven and place the slices in a single layer in the prepared pot. Cover the pot and let the buns rise at room temperature until almost doubled in bulk, about 30 minutes.

Preheat the oven to 400°F. Uncover the pot and bake until the cinnamon rolls are golden brown, 15–20 minutes.

Meanwhile, in the bowl of a stand mixer fitted with the paddle attachment, beat together the cream cheese, the remaining 6 tablespoons butter, confectioners' sugar, and vanilla on medium speed until smooth, 3–4 minutes. Remove the cinnamon rolls from the oven and let cool in the pot on a wire rack for 5 minutes. Spread the icing over the rolls and serve warm.

MAKES 10–12 ROLLS

½ cup plus 1 tablespoon lukewarm (110°–120°F) milk

1½ teaspoons instant or active dry yeast

1 large egg, at room temperature

½ cup unsalted butter, at room temperature

2½ cups all-purpose flour, plus more for dusting

¾ cup firmly packed light brown sugar

Kosher salt

1½ teaspoons ground cinnamon

Zest of 1 orange

¼ lb cream cheese, at room temperature

¾ cup confectioners' sugar

½ teaspoon vanilla extract

Cherry Crumble with White Chocolate–Hazelnut Streusel

You can use pitted fresh cherries instead of frozen, or swap a portion of the cherries for raspberries or strawberries, either fresh or frozen. Taste the filling before topping with the streusel and adjust as needed with more lemon juice or sugar.

For the filling

3 lb frozen cherries

⅓ cup sugar

⅓ cup cornstarch

1 teaspoon ground ginger

1 teaspoon ground cinnamon

Kosher salt

1 tablespoon fresh lemon juice

For the streusel

⅔ cup all-purpose flour

⅔ cup rolled oats

2 tablespoons sugar

1 teaspoon baking powder

Kosher salt

⅔ cup chopped hazelnuts

6 tablespoons unsalted butter, melted and cooled

⅔ cup white chocolate chips

Whipped cream or vanilla ice cream, for serving

Preheat the oven to 375°F.

To make the filling, in a 5-qt dutch oven over medium heat, combine the cherries, sugar, cornstarch, ginger, cinnamon, and ¼ teaspoon salt. Cook, stirring frequently, until thickened, about 10 minutes. Stir in the lemon juice and remove from the heat.

To make the streusel, in a bowl, whisk together the flour, oats, sugar, baking powder, 1 teaspoon salt, and the hazelnuts. Stir in the melted butter until completely incorporated, then stir in the white chocolate chips.

Spread the streusel over the cherry filling in an even layer. Bake until the filling is bubbling and the streusel is toasted and golden brown, 15–20 minutes. Let stand for 10 minutes before serving with whipped cream.

SERVES 6–8

Index

The Dutch Oven Cookbook

Conceived and produced by Weldon Owen, Inc.
in collaboration with Williams-Sonoma, Inc.
3250 Van Ness Avenue, San Francisco, CA 94109

A WELDON OWEN PRODUCTION
1150 Brickyard Cove Road
Richmond, CA 94801
www.weldonowen.com

WELDON OWEN INTERNATIONAL
President & Publisher Roger Shaw
SVP, Sales & Marketing Amy Kaneko
Finance & Operations Director Philip Paulick

Copyright © 2016 Weldon Owen International
and Williams Sonoma, Inc.
All rights reserved, including the right of
reproduction in whole or in part in any form.

Associate Publisher Amy Marr
Project Editor Lesley Bruynesteyn

Creative Director Kelly Booth
Art Director Marisa Kwek
Senior Production Designer
   Rachel Lopez Metzger

Printed in China
First printed in 2016
10 9 8 7 6 5

Production Director Chris Hemesath
Associate Production Director
   Michelle Duggan
Imaging Manager Don Hill

Library of Congress Cataloging-in-Publication
data is available.

ISBN 13: 978-1-68188-146-1
ISBN 10: 1-68188-146-2

Photographer Aubrie Pick
Food Stylist Lillian Kang
Prop Stylist Ethel Brennan

ACKNOWLEDGMENTS

Weldon Owen wishes to thank the following people for their
generous support in producing this book: Kris Balloun, Veronica Laramie,
Rachel Markowitz, Alexis Mersel, Elizabeth Parson, and Miki Vargas